AF211946

ALFRED MERTON

EVERYBODY WRITES

The Ultimate Guide on Writing for Beginners, Learn Writing Tips and the Easy Ways to Write EBooks, Blogs and Other Online Content

Descrierea CIP a Bibliotecii Naţionale a României
ALFRED MERTON
  EVERYBODY WRITES. The Ultimate Guide on Writing for Beginners, Learn Writing Tips and the Easy Ways to Write EBooks, Blogs and Other Online Content – Bucharest: Editura My Ebook, 2021
  ISBN

ALFRED MERTON

EVERYBODY WRITES

The Ultimate Guide on Writing for Beginners, Learn Writing Tips and the Easy Ways to Write EBooks, Blogs and Other Online Content

My Ebook Publishing House
Bucharest, 2021

TABLE OF CONTENTS

CHAPTER 1

BECOMING AN AUTHOR

Writing an ebook is one of the easiest ways to become an author. These days, you don't need a publishing house or literary agent to get published. The Internet and modern software packages have made it possible for anyone who wants to create his/her own ebook. Even if you decide you don't have a knack for writing, there are other ways to put together an informative piece of work that will sell and will help to get you labeled as an expert. All it takes to start is having a passion for or knowledge about some popular niche that you want to market in ebook format.

FINDING YOUR NICHE

People who want to become authors usually have a specialty that they want to pursue. However, it is a wise business owner who finds the hot niches first and then goes out to write about them. This way, you know there already is a market for the ebook before you even put a single word to paper. While you do want to go into something that sets you on fire, there is probably one angle above others that will help it to sell more. Remember that people will buy ebooks because they have a problem that they want solved or they need more information on a specific issue that will enhance their lives. If your passion is jewelry, you may find that an ebook on how to pick out an engagement ring might be a hot topic. You want your niche to be specific enough to attract the demographic you already have as an audience, but not so wide that it seems too broad-based to offer any useful information.

If you're not sure where to start, check out hot topics on popular blogs by going to Technorati.com. See what excites people and what questions people have about a certain topic or dilemma in their lives. Look at the news, see what's on everyone's mind, and try to develop a topic niche that can help address those issues. Right now, economic topics are very much in demand from saving money to making money in a tight economy.

FLAUNT YOUR CREDENTIALS

The author is just as important as the topic, and you want to flaunt your credentials if you have them. Give the reader some idea of why you are especially qualified to write this ebook. Your credentials don't have to be a Ph.D., but they can be some inspiring story that shows why you are the one to help your customers resolve some issue in their lives. Credentials come in many forms, not all of them being academic. They come in life experience, business achievements, and the school of hard knocks. Whatever it is that makes you qualified, make sure your reader knows why you wrote your book.

CHAPTER 2

WRITING IS EASY, RIGHT?

Many people who have never sat down to write an actual article think that writing as a craft is simple. You just start with one word, and you follow that with another. It's also usually all in your native language. How hard can that be, right? Well, once they start to write, they may find that they don't have a clue on where to start. If they've never written an ebook, they may not understand how to properly organize their thoughts so that enough information is conveyed in an easy and highly digestible form for the reader. In fact, once they sit down to look at a blank sheet of paper, they may actually freeze because they have no set plan in place. That's why it's important to sketch out an outline before you start. Let's first take a look at how long an average ebook might be and how to set up chapters to fill the pages.

WHAT'S A GOOD LENGTH?

In general, ebooks can range from 50 to 100 pages. Unlike published books that range in the 200- to 300-page range, ebooks are much shorter since they are electronic in nature and are meant for an audience that isn't reading them like a novel. They are informational mostly, although adding some humor and entertainment is permissible. People who buy ebooks are looking for solutions, not entertainment, and they want it to be informative, not pure fluff. They also want it to be a quick read, as they're used to reading short Web articles or even short reports. For this audience, 50 pages is enough, but never exceed 100 pages.

YOUR OUTLINE

Within those 50 pages, it's common to see about 10 chapter headings. That gives you about five pages for each major topic in your ebook. There's no right or wrong way to divide chapters up, and you can make some longer and others shorter, but on average, most will be five pages long of written text. You can add pictures, but those shouldn't count towards the text. That means that when you sit down to brainstorm your ebook, you will want 10 main headings.

Within those 10 chapter headings, you may end up with several subheadings. These break out your major topic into easily digestible packets of information that people can scan via the table of contents. We will discuss how to automate the creation of the table of contents so that each of those headings and subheadings with corresponding page numbers is inserted at the front of your book. For now, realize that you will need to brainstorm an outline with 10 major points and three or more subheadings each.

CHAPTER 3

FILL IN THE BLANKS

Once you have a good outline, you'll know what topics you need to research more and can spend a little time doing just that. You should become familiar with quick ways to research any topic so that it can speed up the writing process. If you're a walking library of information on your topic, you won't have to spend much time researching anything. However, for those that want to spend a bit more time getting into their subject more, there are a few options before they set pen to paper.

GOOGLE IT

Use keywords that define your niche topic for each chapter to Google new information across the Internet. Almost everyone is familiar with Google's search engine. You can even use the advanced search to limit yourself to recent postings on the Web too to make your information more current. Just be sure not to plagiarize information and to use it solely for research purposes. Be careful about the information on Google, as sources may not be accurate, so it does take some good ability to discern good and bad information via the references offered in each article. Even Wikipedia, a great source for research, is not 100% accurate, since it is updated by everyday people who can and do make mistakes. Consider the source when doing research. This way, you'll be more accurate if you use any facts or figures that are quoted within an article by checking the source too.

ASK AN EXPERT

A great way to put together some valuable information for your readers that you don't know without necessarily doing heavy-duty research is to ask an expert to contribute to your ebook. Of course, there has to be something in it for him/her, but you can do an entire ebook with chapters devoted to him/her discussing a particular topic of interest to your readers. If you promise to let him/her link to his/her products and services within the ebook, and you have a wide enough audience who will be offered the ebook for free, it can be a win-win for everyone. Write it up in an interview format that's very easy to read and nicely segmented. In some cases, the ebook might be a promotional item to help you prod a person into buying something else that you and/or your expert sponsors, so it's not going to be sold, but is going to be given away instead. With so much exposure available to experts trying to sell their products, it will be something that will interest them to help you with it because it will help them sell their products to a new audience.

CHAPTER 4

HOW TO FORMAT EVERYTHING QUICKLY

If you're using Word, you can format your headings and subheadings so that they can be used easily at the end of the creation of your ebook to generate a table of contents (TOC). Depending on the word processing package you are using, there will be different menus that allow you to format the headings. If you start with the idea that your chapter and section headings are going to make up the table of contents, you will know ahead of time to format them as you go along. For now, let's just quickly go over how it's done in Microsoft Word, as this is the most popular word processing program out there.

HEADING STYLES

You will have the option to format text that you highlight in different styles. You can do this from the menu or from the Style box on the formatting tool bar if it's showing. Heading 1 is the style that is used for major chapter headings, while Heading 2 is used for subheadings. To apply a Heading 1 Style, you can do one of the following after selecting the text:

1. Click the Style box and choose Heading 1 as your style to apply.

2. Using the menu, you might try using the Format menu, and under Styles, you will be able to click Apply.

3. Use Ctrl-Shift-S for Word versions earlier than 2007 to get to the Format toolbar where you can apply it with the Style box.

Whatever way your word processing program does this, it's still the same in most word processing programs. In OpenOffice, you will even have Chapter Headings that you can use, which are much larger and which appear like the page headings in this report.

TO INSERT THE TOC

Once you have a few heading styles applied, try to see how they look in a shortened TOC. In a new page near the top of your ebook, before your headings and subheadings, you will place your cursor to insert your TOC. This is done by choosing the Insert command on the main menu of Word. In earlier versions of Word, the submenu you want is "Index and Tables" or "Reference/Index and Tables." Click OK, and it will take your headings, add the page numbers, and put in a TOC for you. If you want to change the look of the TOC, choose to modify it within this command, not from within the ebook.

CHAPTER 5

ADDING PICTURES

Adding pictures breaks up the monotony of an ebook, although they're not entirely necessary. It is nice to include a photo with your ebook cover when you market it, but it's not entirely necessary to add them within the ebook itself. Although they can be very helpful when it comes to certain things, like explaining how to do a particular operation on a computer. Just be sure that the pictures you use are either your own or are licensed to you for the proper usage. Otherwise, you can end up in legal trouble for infringing on someone else's copyright.

SCREEN SHOTS

If you're trying to depict how a certain operation is done on the personal computer, you're in luck! It's a very easy thing to take a screen shot off of any personal computer and embed the picture into your ebook. All you have to do is to hit the <Alt> button at the same time as the <Print Screen> button on your keyboard. The <Alt> button is next to the space bar on the left and the <Print Screen> button is on the top right hand side of your keyboard. Pressing the two together takes a picture of whatever is on your screen and saves it to memory.

You will then want to open any photo processing program or even Paintbrush and paste it into the front screen so that you can edit it there. The way to do that in Paintbrush is to simply choose to edit/paste the information into it after you've opened it. Then, you can crop it and resize it if you need to for use in your ebook. To paste it within your ebook, either copy and paste it or insert it via the word processing program after saving it onto your hard disk.

USING STOCK PHOTO BANKS

There are a number of great stock photo banks out there that allow anyone with a few bucks to download some great photos that they can use for free on their personal sites and for a few bucks in their commercial ventures. The terms of the usage will depend on the photo and the site itself. A few good choices to investigate are http://sxc.hu and Dreamstime.com. You sign up as a member and are able to browse photos by categories and by a number of different keywords. Next time you want a photo of a red sports car, it's as simple as logging in and seeing what's available. The selection is tremendous, and the prices are reasonable. You may be able to use a photo for free if you give credit to the site and photographer, but if you want it just as a photo, you will probably have to pay to use it. However, when you factor in the amount of time it will take you to get the perfect shot of just the right image, it is well worth any investment to get a license and just pay for the privilege of using the photos in your ebook.

CHAPTER 6

FOR THOSE THAT TALK BETTER
THAN THEY WRITE

Some people can go on for hours talking about a subject that they are passionate about, but ask them to write about the same thing, and they freeze. If you're one of those people, don't fret. There are tools available to make it easier for you to take advantage of your immense oral knowledge in such a way that it even lessens the amount of time it takes to create an ebook. They may cost a bit more than just using a computer and keyboard, but it can be a Godsend for those who find themselves literally challenged.

DRAGON NATURALLY SPEAKING

The software that is most used by people to create ebooks orally instead of manually is Dragon Naturally Speaking. The most current standard version is $99. It is a Nuance product that is available at http://www.nuance.com/naturallyspeaking. You can probably get it for less if it's not a physical shipment and is downloaded off of the Internet. Some places offer it for $49.99, but it may be an earlier version. Decide what you need and then order it online.

WHY CHOOSE A VOICE RECOGNITION TOOL?

One reason: speed. The average person can only type 40 words a minute, but they can talk much faster, sometimes up to 120 words per minute. If you are a two-fingered typist, then you are going to be able to write much faster using voice recognition software than if you tried to write it from your head onto the keyboard. You also tend to make mistakes when you're typing, whereas the software will write what you speak, with fewer and fewer mistakes the more that you use it. Most of these won't be spelling mistakes, as it uses its own dictionary, but will be recognition errors. After you use the software for a while, it begins to recognize your words better, and you will have a very easy time writing an ebook just by talking through it.

CHAPTER 7

WHEN YOU CAN'T FILL
IN THE BLANKS

Still lacking inspiration? It's not unusual for people who have never written an ebook to find themselves stuck for words. Don't worry though, because if you find that you can't find the words, there are still other methods that you can use to get the information down on paper. The most important part of writing the ebook is really the topic and the outline. Once you have that done, you have the framework to fill in whether you write the material or not. One way to get the job done, even when you don't do the writing yourself, is to use Private Label Rights (PLR).

WHAT IS PLR?

Private Label Rights is copy written that provides a license to modify and to use that material as your own, even when someone else wrote it. PLR comes in the form of Web articles, reports, and ebooks. PLR is sold to people looking for content that they want to use for different purposes. You can use PLR as is, but it's often better to take some PLR content and modify it so that it isn't an exact duplicate of some other copy bought by some other person too. People can buy PLR ebooks, but they may not follow exactly the outline you've set up. They'll be someone else's ideas of what's important about a topic. Thus, if you want to use PLR content and still have it follow your outline, you'll need to use a different strategy.

BUY PLR ARTICLES

You can buy multiple PLR articles on your chosen subject, tear them up, use different paragraphs, reorder the content into different chapters, and make an ebook out of them. As long as it

26

has a PLR license, you can even modify the content and put your name on it, and it's completely acceptable. It's also a fairly quick way to fill in those blanks when you just can't seem to get the words out.

WHERE TO FIND PLR

You can Google online for "PLR." It's available for sale from different websites, and you'll want to find some that are relevant to your topic. Or you can join PLR membership sites that offer PLR on a variety of topics and use that content to create multiple ebooks on different subjects. The same way you can create an ebook from multiple articles, you can also create separate articles from a PLR ebook. There are lots of uses for PLR, and they're usually available at very cheap prices.

CHAPTER 8

WHAT ABOUT GHOSTWRITERS?

Another popular way of getting a first ebook out is to hire someone to ghostwrite it for you. It may seem like a cop-out, but even people who have already made a name for themselves with their own original research and ideas in published works will hire ghostwriters from time to time. It's a way to reduce the amount of time taken in the writing process, as freelance writers can put together a 50-page ebook in less than a week in some cases and often do it better than if you spent months doing it yourself.

COSTS MORE THAN PLR

Ghostwriting is more expensive than using PLR, as you are paying someone to develop original material and then transfer all rights to you. You can even claim the work as your own after that, but no one else gets the right to publish that content other than you. That's the major difference, and the reason that the pricing is much higher for ghostwritten work than for PLR. You can be assured that you won't be posting anything that anyone else has posted on the Web from the same PLR source you got yours, as it's not PLR, but original copy. While you might only pay a few dollars for an entire PLR ebook, you can be certain that ghostwritten work will cost you dollars per page, not per product.

YOU GET WHAT YOU PAY FOR

Even though the cost is higher, the quality is much higher too. Freelance writers will take the trouble to spell check their work and use correct grammar. They will follow your outline

29

exactly, saving you the time trying to find PLR articles that fit within your framework. Some freelancers are so knowledgeable about their niches that they will even provide you with an outline, and all you have to do is to approve it first. The research is often all in their heads or is available from other jobs. If you ask for a table of contents, they'll provide that too. In general, using a freelance writer is the most highly customizable way to get original copy that you can later claim as your own work.

YOU CAN USE THEM AGAIN

Good freelance writers will actually make you money, even if they cost you more than PLR or a voice recognition software program. That's because you aren't just paying for the words that they write, but also for the information stored in their heads. They come with their own backgrounds that may include information you need, but don't know. They know what's hot in their markets and how to present information so that it is easy to read and that it provides solutions to your customers. Get a good one and keep them to use again and again.

CHAPTER 9

HOW TO HIRE FREELANCE WRITERS

Not everyone that calls himself/herself a freelance writer is going to work for you. Each writer has his/her own level of proficiency and knowledge base. Some will work for some types of work, like short articles, but be unable to deliver ebooks on larger topics that require more in-depth research. Others won't be available when you need them. Your best bet is to start looking now if you think you are going to go about hiring freelance writers on a continual basis. The first thing you want to do is to start looking them up on different job boards, like Elance.com and Freelancer.com.

FREELANCE BOARDS

Elance.com and Freelancer.com (previously called GetAFreelancer.com) are bulletin boards where buyers and sellers of different freelance talent can come and find each other. You can hire freelance writers there, as well as coders and graphic artists. They will allow freelancers to post their profiles online and to bid on projects posted by buyers. You can take a look at any number of projects that are up for bid, and also at the profiles of those who are bidding on them. Once a project is completed, the person is rated by the buyer, and so you also have that feedback that can help you determine whether the person might be a good match for you or not.

TAKE A LOOK AT PROFILES

Take a very good look at each seller profile. They will offer samples of their work so that you can see what their specialty niches are and whether their writing style is close to what you want. It will also give you an idea of how long they've

32

been doing this type of work and what their expected pay rate might be. The pay between freelancers varies greatly, as some have more years of experience and/or specific knowledge of hot niches that puts them in high demand.

START WITH A SMALL PROJECT

Start with a small project that you can post and determine who might be available and who will bid on it for you. Or you can email people whose profiles you like and ask them if they would like to do a private project for you. You don't have to start by putting something up to bid if you find a few profiles that work for you. If you do put it up to bid, you can invite the people you like to bid on it. If they're available, they're more than likely to bid on it. If the project shows that they can handle a larger project, then you can ask them to do the ebook. By doing a smaller project first, you'll get a good idea of whether they will work out for you with a larger project or not.

CHAPTER 10

LOCKING YOUR CONTENT AWAY

You will receive editable content from ghostwriters, from speech recognition software, and even from using PLR. It will be in a popular word processing format that you will not want to sell as is. You have to lock the content away so that people can't take it, use it without paying for the rights to use it, and steal portions of it to put on their websites, to use in their own ebooks, and so forth. You do have to use some safeguards to keep your content safe; after all, it was your money, your time, and your hard work that went into it. If anyone stands to profit from it, it should be you and no one else.

ADOBE ACROBAT READER

This software program is the standard for ebooks and allows anyone with the reader to view .pdf files from their personal computer. The reader itself is free, but the actual Adobe software to create your own .pdf file is expensive. If you intend on doing many books and want many of the features of the Adobe Acrobat line of products, then it can be a sound investment. However, if you just want a straight .pdf file format, there are a variety of ways you can produce the same thing for nothing.

ONLINE PDF CONVERTERS

There are free online .pdf converters available that will allow you to post your content to them and they emailing you back the .pdf version. They may or may not be that compatible with Adobe Acrobat Reader, and you should check to see how the final product looks when opened with Adobe Acrobat Reader. You also want to be sure that it opens in the latest version of the Reader, as this can differ too. It may be a trial-and-error process, as many things can shift in the formatting of the ebook when you convert it from a word processing format to a .pdf format. Be sure to load it and then proofread it for orphaned titles and such on pages that were formatted incorrectly. Much of this can be fixed just by adding additional spacing into the original document and then converting it again.

OPENOFFICE

If you don't want to go through the trouble of doing things back and forth online, and you don't want to pay for Adobe Acrobat for .pdf file creation, you can still use an open source product called OpenOffice to get the option to export to a .pdf file. This is loaded directly onto your personal computer; it has a suite of products similar to Microsoft Office, except that it requires no licensing or sales fees. You can get Openoffice for free at http://www.openoffice.org. Using the word processing program, you can open the file that was sent to you or that was created in another program, and then using the File menu, you can choose the "Export as PDF..." format to get the right kind of file. Once that's done, your file will be protected from people who want to try and copy and paste the information to their sites or products. It won't be possible to do that operation anymore, so they will have to pay you or notify you if they want the copy in text format.

You will receive editable content from ghostwriters, from speech recognition software, and even from using PLR. It will be in a popular word processing format that you will not want to sell as is. You have to lock the content away so that people can't take it, use it without paying for the rights to use it, and steal portions of it to put on their websites, to use in their own ebooks, and so forth. You do have to use some safeguards to keep your content safe; after all, it was your money, your time, and your hard work that went into it. If anyone stands to profit from it, it should be you and no one else.

CHAPTER 11

START WRITING ON A DAILY BASIS

The more you write the better you will become at writing. So, it just makes sense that you want to get into the habit of writing every day. You don't have to start writing pages upon pages each day. Your goal is to form the habit where you sit down at your computer and start typing words into a document or notepad.

You can write about anything. For example, you may want to write about your activities the day before. Start mapping out a business plan or outline blog posts. Write about anything that gets you into the habit of actually writing. You may even want to practice writing short posts which you could then use as content for your social sites.

It may be difficult at first to write every day. Just remember, as with any habit, if you commit to doing this daily you will be writing regularly in less than one month.

Printed by Libri Plureos GmbH in Hamburg, Germany